False Borders

False Borders

Poems by

Sue Budin

© 2022 Sue Budin. All rights reserved.
This material may not be reproduced in any form, published,
reprinted, recorded, performed, broadcast,
rewritten or redistributed without
the explicit permission of Sue Budin.
All such actions are strictly prohibited by law.

Cover design by Shay Culligan
Cover image by John Lloyd

ISBN: 978-1-63980-165-7

Kelsay Books
502 South 1040 East, A-119
American Fork, Utah 84003
Kelsaybooks.com

For John

Acknowledgments

Poems in this book have previously appeared in:

Third Wednesday: "Jigsaw"

Peninsula Poets: "Sally Hawkins Speaks"

Poetica Magazine: "Rest Stop on the Ohio Turnpike"

Meridian Anthology of Contemporary Poetry: "Two Ducks and a Bunny"

Contents

I False Borders

False Borders	15
City	16
Art for Art's Sake	18
Daily Life	19
On Beauty	20
After the Blizzard	21
Markers	22
La Pura Vida Revisited	23
Return Trip	24
Jigsaw	25
Passport, 1954	26

II Intimacies

Synesthesia	29
Sally Hawkins Speaks	30
Remembering An Old Friend	31
Two Ducks and a Bunny	33
Japanese Baskets	34
Aquarium Misnomer	36
I Dream About Weaving	37
Sunset Over K Mart	38
Rest Stop on the Ohio Turnpike	39
Parts of Speech Find New Occupations	41

III Worlds Beyond

The Taurid Swarm	45
Totality	47
Life on Mars	48
Spacecraft	49

On Hearing of the Imminent Crash of a Satellite
   on Earth   50
Einstein's Rings   51
Mercury in Retrograde   52

I
False Borders

False Borders

It's the edges,
those lines we think define us—
skin, words, black lines on maps.

I crossed over one from New Hampshire
to Maine, imagined differences in terrain,
heard the talk of fishing crews,
raw and brash, as they pulled the big ones
from the water. The mountain named Katahdin
cast its shadow across the line.

On the coast of Brazil, people mourn
their loss, those ancestors
brought from Angola and the Congo
to hard labor, the edges of their continent,
once enjoined with Africa,
now ragged edges, an ocean between.
Today, families talk on cell phones,
sending love to distant towers.

Migrants wait under bridges for weeks, months.
Hungry children hide in the gathers of their mothers' skirts,
waiting to enter, crossing rivers, dying in deserts
that were once their own.
Let them in. Let them in.

Imagine the same air between us,
moving first through one body,
then another.
That is a start.

City

Narrow as a
long room,

this alley, this

building that
blackens the concrete below
with its shadow
spilling out

onto the street
where parked cars
settle in, motors silent,
as the city talks and talks.

Bulldozer, drill reverberate,
agitate the brittle leaves
hanging on in late fall.

Darkness under elevated trains
at noon leads workers astray
in this eternal dusk.

Trash piles up, overflows
the rim.

Birds sing on wires,
telegraphing messages of hope
and the boy dances in circles
beneath the broken neon sign.

His mother sweeps the steps,
each stroke, a steadying
in the golden light of late afternoon
when windows high above them
glow with promises.

Art for Art's Sake

Creased
folded
once laid out flat
once a bag
holding a container
of soup and bread.
Now, accordioned,
painted, still
a bag
but different
as in art—
objects stripped
of function,
no longer
holding soup
and bread
or even crumbs, only
colored folds—
What you can do
with brown paper
in winter when
cold seeps through
the cracks, stiff fingers
needing the stretch
and pull that cutting,
folding paper
brings.

Daily Life

> After the painting, *Magpie on the Gallows*
> —Peter Brueghel, The Elder

Who is to say, after the hanging,
whether the bird, black and raucous,
should perch on the wooden beam
while peasants dance below?

Death becomes another task
like hauling wheat or laying stone.
After any labor, the villagers dance

in relief, celebrating joy or sorrow
on the cracked canvas where the magpie
is a black speck, hardly noticeable

but for the title and what it means
to us who view the painted scene,
consider what appears indifference.

Meanwhile, dancers circle,
hold hands and kick their feet, the woman's
red skirt, white veil, stark against the muted browns
of tree and field.

On Beauty

Torn posters advertise shoe polish, Piel's Beer, and a diner
selling *Home Made Pies*.
When the wall next door was torn away,
these appeared, along with faded script,
its flourishes barely there.

A painting of a woman stretched along the highest bricks
seduces with Cola. A pink-cheeked baby sucks on a bottle.
Damp ringlets encircle her face.
Pocked surfaces reveal these tattoos: histories
in jagged squares, broken lines.

Ruby lips on chipped stone still show their luster.
The shoe without a heel and the child missing one leg
are left disabled in the peeling paint of past generations.
Crumbling corners meet, expose healing tonics, fenders
of a 1950's Buick, the Rexall Drugstore sign plastered over,
only its edges revealing

all this beauty, fragments made whole in my seeing.
Stories patinaed with age survive amid the rubble.

The building next door with its gold doors, sculpted entry,
throws its shadow on the wall in the city where I was a child, then

and now, looking up.

After the Blizzard

Deep snow covers the roads.
No one travels. A field of white
erases manufactured boundaries.

Houses retreat to the tree line.
Loose clapboards bang against each other.
Windows rattle in their casings.

Inside, a woman stirs a meaty stew.
The dog stays by the door, no memory
of frozen paws, still wanting to go out.

Snowplows etch lines in the whiteness,
wide enough to let the truck through.
Icicles weep in their melting.

Everyone feels it, this reluctance to return
to roads, commerce, the treble of demands,
excuses, arguments with winners and losers.

Light diffuses, turns fences into lace,
the handiwork of a careful artist, hand steady,
tracing split rails in the snow.

Markers

On Independence Day, streaks of colored light
burst into a sky blistered with millions of stars
while across an ocean,
bombs crumble monuments in Mosul,
bloody the bodies of children in Aleppo,
leave mothers wailing, men digging through the cracks
for survivors.

Americans cheer each sizzle, each shower of
petals blooming in the blackness.
In the cool night grass, lovers lean
against each other, the boom
of the grand finale safely held in their chests.

After celebration,
lawn chairs are collapsed, blankets gathered.
Families leave a trail of burned-out sparklers,
stomped-on cups, a baby's shoe, not unlike

the vestiges of battle on a dusty street, sun
beating down on a red baseball cap,
one-armed doll
lying in the rubble.

La Pura Vida Revisited

Away from the great blue heron, snowy egret, long necked anhinga,
the streets of San Jose are dusty, busy with traffic.
People wait for buses.
We cross a bridge to a park where people roller blade.
Families sit on benches.
Children draw in dust at their feet.

Like in any American city, we tread the same concrete,
watch the tired faces of the working poor, breathe in car exhaust.
Houses painted pink and orange stand behind
razor wire and locked gates in this country
where no army lures young men to war.

Up the mountain roads, Poaz in the north pours steam into the air.
Behind railings, we look down into a crater, ponder eons
of continuous eruptions. In the valley, hummingbirds,
their wings a blur, sip sweet water from feeders. Like magma
cooled, then heated,
they are ancient habitants but with no time to lose.

At the river, alligators lay on logs where only their eyes betray them.
Everywhere, there are rumblings, invisible vibrations—
in the city's streets, the forest where a sudden streak of white,
the screech of monkeys in the trees, are signs of danger,
prey and predator meeting unexpectedly in corners.

Return Trip

Between Happy Valley and Pittsburgh, a few miles off Route 80,
there's a small town with a levee where people walk at sunset.
To get there, we walk past a yard where four growling canines
run to the fence. "Beware of dogs," the sign says.

Streetlights hold pictures of fallen heroes. On porches,
American flags flap in the gritty wind.
Restaurants say, "No dogs allowed."
We glance into a glaring, fluorescent lit room with an unmade bed.
In the next building is a costume shop of princess dresses.
At the family restaurant, one table is filled.

Shuttered storefronts line the block.
A bar on each corner is still open, music blaring
through closed doors. We cross a ragged crack in crumbling cement,
smell cigarette ash in doorways.
These summer days are long between silent morning
and a troubled night.

We walk our dog back to the Best Western.
A kind woman who works at the motel
pets my dog and tells me about her three Boston terriers.
At 9 p.m., pizza tastes okay with beer.

I imagine a young mother living in this town.
She sings to her sleepy child. The single window
in the room holds the moon, covering them
in its glow.

Jigsaw

Is it the edge of cloud above the lake
or the petals of the roses the girl
holds in her hand?

Most pieces interlock but these —
the size of the first joint of my thumb
elude me,

their edges like the rounded juts of
land hugging the coves
where waves bring gifts of kelp,
skeletons of fish, shattered whelks.

I imagine standing there,
my feet puzzling out the borders where
my fingers have tired of walking,
looking for solutions, the last pieces
fitting in so tightly with the rest.
But is this an empty comfort?
The closing of seams?
The answer that balances an equation?

I seek the hole, the ravel,
the empty space not filled.
I toss the pieces wildly,
revel in the mystery of
what remains incomplete
in the picture of a girl in a rowboat
who holds a cloud of roses,
looks back at the shore she's left behind,
the fractured sky,
her uncertain future.

Passport, 1954

(On a painting of the same name by Helen Frankenthaler)

Blue is border, river, wall.
Getting past or over is difficult.
Some drown.
Others turn away, go home.

Passion or want brings a flush,
adds a tinge of guilt, remorse.
Red and blue bleed into one another
as if telling their sorrows.
Some colors have always been illegal,
especially orange.

How can any of these hues
ever pass through blue who
swallows them all, its mouth so deep
even the stars fall through?

II
Intimacies

Synesthesia

B.B. King plays blue notes,
blue like late summer plums,
juice running down the woman's chin
while he fills the room with
love he pulls from his guitar.
She tongues the crimson contour
of his riffs, falls in the well of sound
that brings her down, down
into the liquid swell of her loneliness.

She grabs the collar of the downbeat
at the end of *Sweet Little Angel*
and pulls it toward her.

There Must Be a Better World Somewhere,
he sings, brushing indigo along the wall.
She feels a chill as once forbidden words
hover and descend, her white dress
marked with flagged notes.

She breathes in Delta breezes,
swims the muddy river till
the air turns gold.

Sally Hawkins Speaks

(Homage to her role in *The Shape of Water*)

Is it the tilt of lips,
the stars emerging
from the centers of her eyes
when she traces movements
of the creature's hands on the glass
with her own?

The language of love
has no boundaries as she places
eggs on the edge of the pool,
precarious ovals he grabs,
then handles tenderly, swallows
with gratitude, gurgles a reply,

that being mute, she understands. They speak
and listen with their hands, their eyes,
their mouths. Their bodies beckon
and redeem, lean toward the other.
She knows she must free him as

she must free herself. In the water,
his scales shimmer, her hair whips
behind her. She is blessed, brought back
to life, her radiance lighting up the
dark drag of current, her voice at last
heard as singing, his reptilian skin
stroked like a jewel.

Remembering An Old Friend

The snow touch takes us all.
It is the innocence of such spontaneous dance
that brings our fall. (Her words)

She wrote those lines
the year we tucked subversive notes
in tomes of Shakespeare's plays,
laughed till we cried
at the sound of words repeated till
they made no sense.

On the outside, she was
fun to be around
but her written words cut
like icicles about to fall.

This January morning
after days of a deep freeze,
the snow dazzles.
I think of her, the pain she was in
to write such lines on beauty
and its quick demise, the folly
of our faith in worn out symbols
like the purity of snow or rain
to wash away our sins when

behind the shimmering curtain,
came the monster of truth,
snag-toothed, greedy,
stomping on the freshly fallen snow
as if it were our souls.

Where is she now
and what does she believe
about the snow? Like me,
does she see it as a freshening
in winter, softening the edges,
covering the gray, reflecting light?

If she lives near mountains,
does she calm herself with tea,
looking out at snowy peaks,
or in a city, look down at a red
fire hydrant with a white cap,
maybe write about the footprints
of pigeons, their circular patterns,
how a child follows, sinks her hands
in frozen crystals, not knowing
and delighting that it's cold.

Two Ducks and a Bunny

(For Jeannie)

I saw them in the park tonight.
If I believe in signs, then these
are good ones. So is
the lush grass after days of rain
and the bell tower backlit by evening sun.

They've inserted a tube in your chest,
this after weeks of slow recovery
as the new marrow worked its way
through your blood stream like
ducks moved along by a fast-moving river.

These ducks sit in the middle of a
soccer field, no water near except
the puddles left from storms. They seem
content as does the rabbit eating stems of
dandelion. It doesn't move as I approach.

Maybe this walking will help
as I breathe in the live green cells,
my lungs filling extra for you

as the ducks waddle, their plump chests
lifted high. Why is there this fullness in me
as if the danger your life is in brings me round
to what is true and pure—
a park at dusk,
children swinging, and the moon
just beginning to rise.

Japanese Baskets*

Eddying water

Lapwings swoop,
barely skim the water.
Trees sigh their branches down,
comb the river back.

Conversation with bamboo

His fingers bend the supple wood
in and out.
Like gentle lovers.
He and bamboo touch—
let go.

Round mingled hearts

Two bowls.
One rests inside the other,
so comfortable they barely notice
where one begins
the other ends.

River of cherry blossoms

How they fall—
these pink buds on a wet scroll
moving, clear—
the grey stones watch.

Flower basket in the form of a cocoon

Emergent, stretching in its sleep
the bamboo grows, leaves the form
and makes its own
with the help of his hands.

Shimmering of heated air

Hexagons of light—
warm rooms you can go to,
lie inside of,
your bones falling away
in a hive of liquid gold.

Sound of the whirlpool

Round, round and
down into fallen leaves,
river bottom
silence.

Shell of a cicada

Inside the carapace
memory of clicking legs,
heat of summer.
You crawl inside the shell,
hear nothing.

---

*Italicized titles of the baskets are by the artist, master basket maker, Hiroshima Kazuo.

Aquarium Misnomer

Not jelly, nor fish,
this orange parachute
pulsates, aviates,
deviates from what we know
of this world.

This is *other*. Its lacy strands
thread the water, each in-and-out
breath, a jet propulsion.

Looking through the glass, I'm struck
by some forbidden intimacy—to see
through to the heart and its beating—
what we fear most—
an opening, then
a closing, clearly seen—
what all creatures are made for—

A blossoming

A floating

Untethered, barely there
but there, its movement
like the waves, its beat
strong, unending, un
ending.

I Dream About Weaving

In Progresso, on the Yucatan Peninsula,
a woman wove a hammock on a handmade loom.
Her fingers moved the strings
under over, over under.

Returning to the north, I tie it in the shade
between two oaks, let the weight of my body,
the push of my foot on the ground
swing the webbed cocoon, rock me into sleep.

After years, the edges fray.
I take two strands, and tie them together,
then another and another,
each knot a way to relive the day
I stowed the hammock in a canvas bag,
ate fish hauled just that morning from the sea,
drank cold cerveza on a shaded patio.

At times, all one has
is the tying of knots, threads gathered,
cut, secured, no fringe raveling,
bringing the comfort of completion
to a mind tired of loose ends, a body
slowly swinging in the shade where

under heavy lidded eyes, I'm there again—
the span of white-washed walls,
the sea. On the edge of land,
water curls around me,
tectonic plates collide beneath me.

The earth with all its jagged borders,
coasts and reefs remains as one
with separate strands.

Sunset Over K Mart

An orange globe rests on the roof shingles
of the store advertising Blue Light Specials.
In the aisles, people are blind to colors
spreading above them, sun spreading rays
of scarlet and bronze in a tired sky
ready for night.

Inside, flowers bloom on Martha Stewart linens.
Fluorescent reflections mark bottles of hand sanitizer,
club soda.

My car window down,
I drink in the splendor of vermillion dusk
impartial to big box stores and concrete,
crowning any surface where it lands,
settling and spreading crepuscular light,
blessing shoppers pushing carts in the parking lot.

Sun glows on their faces in the sudden chill,
dark closing in.

Rest Stop on the Ohio Turnpike

He emerges like a snail from
the shell of his blue Toyota
on a cold February day.
Holding his prayer book
and kissing the fringe of his shawl,
he dovens, bowing before G-d.

I can't hear the words he chants.
Enclosed in my car, the heat blasting,
I watch him pray in a short-sleeved tee
in the biting wind.

I am reminded of my past,
the ancestry I shook off like the tillit
he pulls around him, so sacred a cloth
that when not in use is tenderly folded
into a small square and laid in a velvet pouch.

Great Grandfather Shamson kissed the cloth daily.
Years later, my father closed the store Good Friday afternoon
to please the Catholic customers
but stayed open on Passover.

I learned to say, "Hear Oh Israel, The Lord our G-d.
The Lord is one." I longed to be as one,
craved something sweet that sweets would not satisfy
but pulled myself away, the story of a lost people
too great for me to bear—blood spilled
over land, the bitterness of mothers.

In the parking lot
the man is still there as I drive away.
I will miss his devotions, will remember
what he gave me on a gray morning in Ohio,
the two of us enfolded in a moment,
the prayer shawl gathering up what was lost.

Parts of Speech Find New Occupations

If I could eminence the sky,
hold it in great esteem,
verb the noun as in
queening the crown or
dooring the way, then
what is solid will melt
and move. What is liquid
will gel. Boundaries
will soften.

I body the house and
walls implode.
I pillar clouds and
wharf the harbor.
I body my body
against the push and pull
of waves that tide
the in and outness of
slumbered breathing.

III
Worlds Beyond

The Taurid Swarm

> "A fair dash of serendipity will be needed to catch a glimpse of it."
> —Dr. Tony Phillips

Not of bees but of meteors,
exploding fireballs of accumulated dust
and gravel, crashing into earth.

In 1908, a rock, 40 meters wide, fell from the sky,
burst into flame in the Tunguska River, Russia,
and destroyed a forest.

At times, you and I are bent on destruction
of our inner solar system. All these years
we've argued, then made up, the hard rock
melting between us.

We feel safe again but occluded, our vision
too focused on a solution.
Out of the corners of our eyes,
flashes of light break our fragile peace
into pieces.

We pick up fragments, make irregular mosaics
from shards of color, no shapes lining up.

Astronomers make predictions of future explosions.
We fail in following trajectories.

When the meteor nears earth, we may cling
to each other or spring apart, welcoming
what comes, unexpected, like a fireball
destroying old growth in a Russian forest,

or let the ground lie fallow, undisturbed—
the gaunt trees close, entangled.

"The Taurid swarm is a dense cluster of meteors within the Taurid meteor stream. Earth periodically passes through the Taurid swarm, and it is one of the three space phenomena that could result in a catastrophic collision."
Source: CBS News.com

Totality

The moon's full coverage of the sun or
the sum of everything. What is entire
becomes famous like a Broadway star
as if completeness were perfection when

uncommon beauty lies in the unfinished line,
the half-sewn hem, the trail of crumbs
that ends before the forest.

Unknown histories, stuttered arguments
make for wonder. Anima, Animas—
the secrets that live inside us, the ghosts
that leave smudges on the walls.

The dark disappears into dawn.
The sun has never met its shadow.
The moon halves and quarters, disappears.
The ragged sound of coronal ejections
serenades us with explosive flares that break and twist,
discordant, with random stops and starts
seeding the temporary dusk of afternoon.

Life on Mars

On the red planet
there are gullies, ridges, places
where nothing can grow.
The only movement is the windstorms
that cover everything in a red film
spreading like a stain,
difficult to wash away but
picked off, piece by piece
until the land is clear, becomes water,
a river, an ocean, a history
of small creatures learning
how to breathe. Their pointed gills
stretch along their sides,
reminders of millennia of waves,
tempests, the movement of mountains.
Sounds explode in ears shaped like
the furled extremities of interplanetary beings.

If only we could listen.
If only we could blast open the horizon,
that line between sea and sky
that divides us, we might discover
newer habitations where we stretch,
finger the false borders of the universe
as water streams through our hands.

Spacecraft

It flew past Pluto last July when
scientists discovered what appeared
"a frozen lake." Because of "tilt,"
they said, extreme compared to Earth,
making this remote place "tropical."

Imagine palm trees, Pina Coladas,
but with temperatures still polar.
There won't be any rush unless
the need for solitude is a split hair
from death. Flat plains, mesas, the "interplay
of different ices" calls the lone traveler
to appreciate its "heart-shaped region,
Tombaugh Regio," the left half
made of snow, the right, of ice,
the mixing of the two erupting then
settling into mountains, one rising from the surface,
its ridge a ninety mile walk from end to end,
the size of a small town.
Girdled in its middle is the warmer though still frigid zone
where a frozen heart can melt,
snow and ice so distant, like a memory of coldness,
a shivering along the body.

Above, the moon of Charon and three others spin on their axes.

Pluto lies in darkness, embraced by a faithless lover
there and not there as the giant orb and its four moons spin,
the two sides of her heart exchanging blood, pulsing
like the water at the bottom of a frozen lake.

On Hearing of the Imminent Crash of a Satellite on Earth

They said they didn't know where it would fall.
There are thousands in the sky.
Like slow motion cephalopods
they float through the dark, star-pricked sky,
their tarnished bodies, each moveable part
appearing so deceptively light.

I sometimes think of meteors crashing into Earth
but not too often. How would I survive
with catastrophe always in mind? It's enough
to contemplate slow growing mold
or the rising incidence of encephalitis in North America.

But I still imagine those lights
blinking in irregular patterns in the heavens
with no brain to contemplate their own demise
while below billions of us scramble like frantic bees
seeking nectar in a grey metropolis

where if only time slowed to the speed of lips
forming words: lovers wrapped in each other's arms,
then each moving thing in space would, like a time lapse,
set its speed to match the undulating praise of lovemaking

and land its cargo gently in a field of sunflowers
all waving their faces in the same direction.

Einstein's Rings

"... the invisible form of matter ..."

It's so big
thought to make up the mass of the universe
so big
that light- when it bounces off
bends, forms rings named after him
who defined that relation
Einstein– a name of
        Holocaust survivor?
        Polish tailor?
        The dreamy but demented taxi driver
        who sings Yiddish love songs
        driving through Manhattan?

And what *does* it matter?
Almost the new year
and those rings are still as far away
as your hands.

It is through this thick membrane of air
                      of silence
                      of unholy thoughts

I must come to reach what
does matter, this matter (of love)
that will hold your light
        break the ring
        let me enter

fold inside the dark cusp
        with you and
out the other side.

Mercury in Retrograde

According to astrologers,
Mercury is out of line.
There's a wobble off the orbit
which may cause, they say,
upsets in binary code, unforeseen storms
tumbling glasses off of shelves.

Astronomers stay calm, draw dotted lines
that form a circle of petals, a flower born
of rebel paths.

Something happens when we go astray.
A letter sending dire news falls beside the curb,
is never read.

Life goes on in the yellow center
of the hyacinth.

Money's found in pockets.
The news read upside down is hopeful.
Shards of glass fly out of the boy's eyes*
and love reappears.

Mercury, fleet footed messenger,
you with silver wings—stray off the path.

*Kai from Andersen's *The Snow Queen*

About the Author

Sue Budin lives in Ann Arbor, MI. She retired as a librarian from the public library, where, as part of her job, she led writing workshops for children and teens. She has been writing poetry for many years and has been published in a variety of journals, including *Meridian Anthology of Contemporary Poetry, Poetica, Ibbetson Street Press, and Earth's Daughters*. Her interest in ekphrastic poetry led her to co-lead a workshop at a local art gallery where participants wrote pieces inspired by art. She currently is a docent at the University of Michigan Museum of Art, where she tries to incorporate writing into her work with visiting school groups. She lives with her husband, likes to garden, weather permitting, and enjoys watching British murder mysteries.

www.ingramcontent.com/pod-product-compliance
Lightning Source LLC
Chambersburg PA
CBHW031206160426
43193CB00008B/526